You Are There!

Ancient CHINA

305 BC

Curtis Slepian, M.A.

Consultants

Timothy Rasinski, Ph.D.
Kent State University

Lori Oczkus, M.A.
Literacy Consultant

Publishing Credits

Rachelle Cracchiolo, M.S.Ed., *Publisher*
Conni Medina, M.A.Ed., *Managing Editor*
Dona Herweck Rice, *Series Developer*
Emily R. Smith, M.A.Ed., *Content Director*
Stephanie Bernard and Seth Rogers, *Editors*
Robin Erickson, *Multimedia Designer*

Image Credits: p.11 De Agostini Picture Library/Getty Images; p.15 Science & Society Picture Library/Getty Images; p.17 Olivier CHOUCHANA/Gamma-Rapho via Getty Images; p.18 (top) Legacy of JA Bierens de Haan, Amsterdam, (bottom) Ivy Close Images / Alamy; p.19 (top) Illustration by Timothy J. Bradley, (bottom) Ivy Close Images / Alamy; All other images from iStock and/or Shutterstock.

Teacher Created Materials
5301 Oceanus Drive
Huntington Beach, CA 92649-1030
http://www.tcmpub.com

ISBN 978-1-4938-3601-7

Printed in Malaysia.THU001.50393

Table of Contents

At the Center of the World

Open your eyes and take a deep breath. You have arrived in southern China in 305 BC! The green landscape is dotted with villages and towns, and passing you are people in tunics and robes. Some men have their hair twisted into long ponytails, while others wear unusual hats. Farmers brush by you, transporting fresh crops in wheelbarrows. Exploring China is going to be an awesome adventure!

The first person you meet eyes you suspiciously and asks if you are a **barbarian**—a person who lives in an area surrounding China and who doesn't share Chinese culture. She claims that beyond barbarian lands live unknown monsters.

How It Began

According to the Chinese story of creation, a giant egg appeared in nothingness more than 18,000 years ago. Inside the egg was a spirit named Pan Gu. When he stood, the egg split. One part became the sky and the other the ground. When Pan Gu died, his body turned into just about every feature in the universe, from rivers to stars.

Checking Out China

You may be the only person in China who knows what the outside world is like. You studied a map of China before this trip. You know that to China's west are impassable mountain chains and the 10,000-foot (3.05-kilometer) high Plateau of Tibet. To the north are huge deserts, such as the Gobi Desert. In the south, jungles form a natural barrier. To the east, the Pacific Ocean is a seemingly endless expanse.

You better get a move on! It's time to check out this fantastic place. A farmer carrying a hoe points out a city in the distance. That's where you head.

Population Explosion

The population of ancient China was about 20 million in 305 BC. That was greater than all of Europe. Today, China's population is about 1.3 billion. That's the most of any country in the world! In fact, China has about 20 percent of the whole world's population.

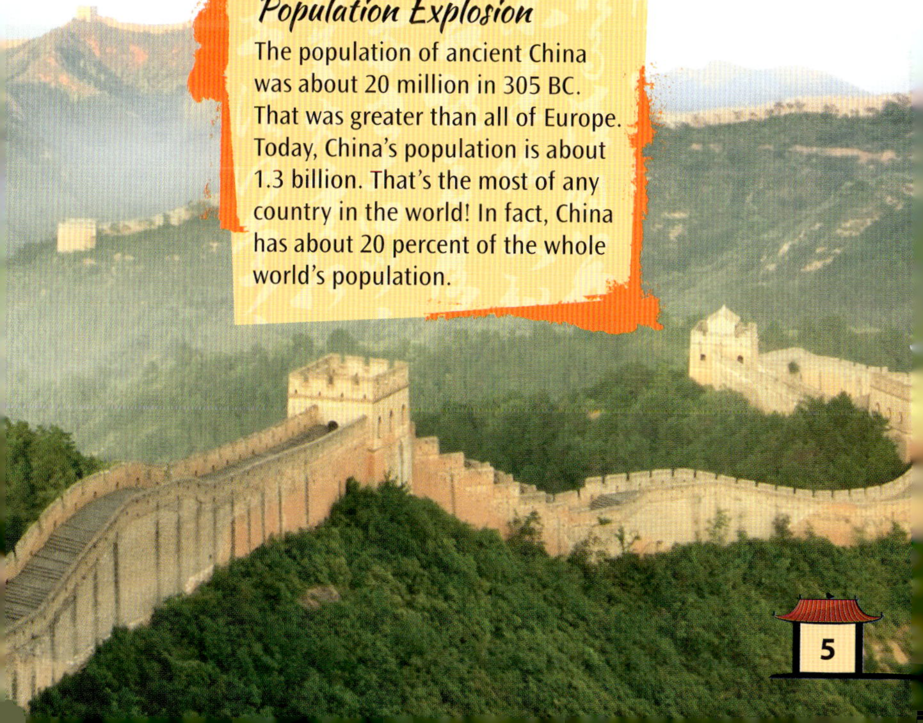

Looking Back

You enter a crowded city near the Yangtze River, China's longest river. The town is full of new sights, smells, and sounds. You feel bewildered. An old man introduces himself as a **scholar** and offers to give you a quick history lesson. He claims that the first true rulers of China were the Three **Sovereigns** and Five Emperors. They were half god and half human. They discovered fire, agriculture, medicine, and writing.

The First Dynasties

China measures its history in dynasties instead of centuries. Every dynasty has its own separate history and culture. The chart shows China's history up to the Qin dynasty. The Qin is considered the first empire because it united all of China.

The scholar says the Xia was China's first **dynasty**. Although he has little evidence, the scholar tells you that it was supposedly the first dynasty to pass the kingship down to family members. The Xia dynasty lasted for nearly 500 years. Over that time, it included the reigns of 17 rulers.

The Shang dynasty followed, and the scholar shows you an ancient **bronze** jar and an animal bone with writings that mention it. The Shang ruled in northern China, where most of the country's population still lives. The Shang kings performed rituals so the spirits of their ancestors would bring them good fortune. This is called *ancestor worship*. But the Shang was conquered by another kingdom called the Zhou.

Years	Period	Major Accomplishments
10,000–2000 BC	Prehistoric	first settlements, beginning of agriculture, decorated pottery, silk production
2100–1600 BC	Xia Dynasty	flood control, cast bronze objects, crafted jade, ruled by heredity
1600–1046 BC	Shang Dynasty	writing, produced bronze weapons and vessels, invented accurate calendar, centralized government
1046–256 BC	Zhou Dynasty	government bureaucracy, iron used in warfare and farm tools, agricultural production, large new cities, metal coins, horseback riding, music and poetry
1046–771 BC	Western Zhou	absorbed barbarians into Chinese culture, increased government efficiency
771–256 BC	Eastern Zhou	intellectual and technical innovations from architecture to warfare to philosophy
770–475 BC	Spring and Autumn	large-scale public works (including city walls, canals, reservoirs, and roads)
475–221 BC	Warring States	innovations in warfare, great thinkers and teachers
221–206 BC	Qin Dynasty	united all of China

STOP! THINK...

Use the chart to answer these questions:

- Which period seems the most warlike? How can you tell?
- Why do you think agriculture increased during the Zhou dynasty?
- Why is China's history described through dynasties rather than centuries?

ancient Chinese water jug

Zhou in Charge

You're in a city ruled by the Zhou. The Zhou kings have been in charge for 741 years. The scholar proudly describes their great accomplishments. They've built many towns and cities, like this one. And, he brags, the central government has brought order to the land—until recently. You've arrived during a pretty troubled time. People are calling it the Warring States period. The states, ruled by king-appointed nobles, are constantly in conflict. As you stroll around town, you notice signs of war.

The Great Wall of China

Wall to Wall

The Great Wall of China started out as many not-so-great walls. Several kingdoms built walls of pounded earth and stones at their borders to protect against invaders. The walls were later strengthened and connected to create the Great Wall.

Battle Stations

You can tell the city is on constant alert. Surrounding it are walls with watchtowers manned by soldiers. Other soldiers patrol the countryside on horseback. Just as you pass within the city walls, you're knocked down by a horse-drawn chariot with three riders.

The driver tells you that the nobles raise massive armies made up of as many as 100,000 soldiers, who are all peasants. Men in chariots often lead the armies into battle. One soldier drives, another holds a long spear, and a third shoots a bow.

The driver of the chariot explains, that over the years, Chinese innovations have made war more deadly. Armies have started using **cavalry**. The Zhou people produced the first iron weapons, such as the iron-tipped, eight-foot (2.44-meter) spear that is handed to you. It's so heavy you almost can't lift it. The invention of the **crossbow** has made it easier to shoot arrows. But the chariot's bowman prefers his old-fashioned bow, which looks just as dangerous.

THINK LINK

- What is special about ancient China?
- Why is it important to know about China's history?
- What are ways people can learn about a country's past?

From Rags to Riches

As you continue on your visit, you come across a group of merchants selling vegetables and grains. They explain that farmers are 80 percent of the population and feed the other 20 percent. In dry northern China, farmers grow wheat and **millet**. These grains make noodles and dumplings. The merchants explain that rice grows abundantly in the warm, wet climate of the south.

The chariot driver gives you a lift to a farming village, which is a group of simple houses with **thatched** roofs, dirt floors, and no furniture. Whole families live in single rooms. When you enter a house, it's a tight squeeze.

The family is China's main social unit. The country's ruler is considered the father of his kingdom, and the subjects are his children.

Pick-Up Sticks

The chopsticks you use to eat a tasty meal were invented during the Shang dynasty. To save on fuel, people cut up food into small pieces so the ingredients cooked faster. Bamboo chopsticks made it easy to both stir food in the pan and pick up the small chunks to eat.

reconstruction of a hut in the ancient village of Banpo, China

Noodling Around

In China, scientists unearthed what they believe is an old noodle. They think it was made around 2000 BC, making it the world's oldest noodle!

On the Farm

The Zhou king has divided his land into territories, each ruled by a **nobleman**. You follow the farmer from dawn to dusk as he works on plots, including one reserved for the local nobleman, who receives whatever is grown there.

You are amazed at the self-sufficiency of the farmer and his family. You try on the shoes they made from straw and the rough clothes woven from **hemp**. They eat the grains and vegetables they grow and the chickens and pigs they raise. You travel along with the oldest son as he hunts for small animals.

Rice Time

You accompany several farmers and their sons to rice paddies. The fields have been plowed and flooded with water from a nearby canal. You come upon rows of peasants planting rice seedlings. At harvest time, the fields will be drained of water, permitting the farmers to gather the rice plants. They do this work by hand. It's an **arduous** task.

As you work, you begin to talk to one of the nearby farmers about his life. The farmer's existence is **oppressive** in many ways. Weather, such as a drought or flood, can destroy a harvest without warning. Peasants like him must serve as **infantry** in the army, as well as toil on public projects, such as road construction. Life is not easy for peasants in this time period!

Funky Fertilizer

Most farmers use the waste of animals as fertilizer. The fertilizer helps crops grow. But farm animals were scarce in ancient China. So farmers had to use human waste, called "night soil," as fertilizer.

Farmers use terraces like these to grow rice on steep hills.

Fancy Threads

At the end of a long, exhausting day of work, you head home with the farmers. The farmers' wives are making silk. They've kept thousands of silkworms at the right temperature, while feeding them the leaves of mulberry plants. Each worm spins a silk thread around its body to form a cocoon, which is heated to kill the silkworm inside. The women are unraveling silk fibers onto spools.

You try your hand at it, and when you finish, your hands ache. Each cocoon is made of a single fiber that can stretch longer than 2,600 feet (800 meters)! These silk threads will be woven into clothing that only kings and nobles are allowed to wear.

Valuable Secrets

In later centuries, silk became prized in Europe. Because silk was so valuable, the emperors of China kept the silk-making process a secret. Anyone caught giving away the secrets or taking silkworms out of China was sentenced to death! These strict laws protected the secrets of Chinese silk-making for hundreds of years.

Living Like a King

From the farm, you hike along dusty roads to the capital city. As you approach, its 33-foot (10-meter) high wall looms above you. Just outside the city, bustling stalls have food, clothing, farm implements, and household goods to be sold to commoners. You watch **artisans** carving jade, a hard green stone, into masks, bracelets, and other ornaments.

You pass through tall gates to reach the palace. There are impressive gardens, religious temples, and government buildings. The king's quarters have tile roofs and ornately carved wooden **pillars**. You ask a worker why the buildings are raised on platforms. He points upward and says that it rains a lot.

Royal Duties

In a great hall, you watch servants and slaves attend to the king, while nobles mill about. They wear elegant silk clothes and cloth slippers or leather shoes. A **bureaucrat** says the king leaves the governing to paid officials like him, and he mentions the king's main concern is performing rituals to keep his world in harmony. The bureaucrat whispers to you that the king wastes too much money on himself.

When the king goes to his temple to pray, you watch from a distance. As an offering, he places food in a bronze **vessel**. You hear him ask for a good harvest—and for the loyalty of his nobles.

Money Matters

The Zhou invented metal coins. The first ones were shaped like knives and farm tools, such as spades. Eventually, round metal coins were introduced with holes in the middles so they could be strung together.

An Unkingly King

According to legend, a king once lit a fire to signal that he needed help from his nobleman. But the king was pulling a prank to amuse his queen. When the nobles arrived with troops, the king and queen laughed. The next time the king lit the signal fire, he was in real danger, but no one came to help. This was the end of the king and his queen.

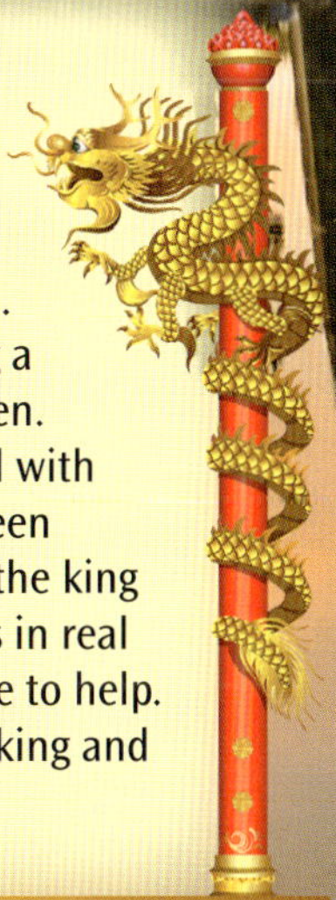

Bright Ideas

Qu Yuan, China's most famous poet, makes an appearance at the royal court. He recites verses criticizing the king. When you applaud, Qu Yuan comes over and complains about the political situation. The king is weak, and warfare is constant. The good news is that many great thinkers are trying to figure out how to bring peace and stability.

Qu Yuan tells you that his favorite **philosopher** is Confucius. Confucius thought society should return to the values of the good old days. He thought people should go back to respecting authority. Confucius also wanted people to treat each other with kindness and respect.

dragon boats

Mega Confucius

In 2011, Artist Zhang Huan created a giant statue of Confucius sitting in a pool of water. The statue is very realistic looking. The artist says the theme of his sculpture is the role spirituality plays in modern China.

Know Your Place

Confucius didn't believe in "doing your own thing," insists Qu Yuan. Instead, China can only achieve peace and harmony when each person knows his or her place in society. A king should be a king, his subjects should be subjects, the father a father, the son a son. Children should obey parents. "Isn't that the natural order of things?" asks Qu Yuan. When you don't reply, the poet offers one final nugget of **Confucianism**, "The people will be loyal to a king only if he is a morally good person. The king should respect his subjects." And with that, Qu Yuan stands up and recites more poetry.

For a Poet

China's annual Dragon Boat Festival is a boat race that honors the memory of Qu Yuan. The poet was so angry by the corruption and needless warfare that he threw himself into a river. Villagers in boats tried desperately to rescue him but failed.

The Master's Voice

You leave the court and sit beside a royal pond stocked with fish. Several teachers of Confucianism have gathered here to have an earnest discussion about Confucius's life with anyone who will listen. You learn that Confucius was born in 551 BC and died in 479 BC. He traveled to royal courts to teach his ideas about how people and rulers should behave. His **disciples** recorded his sayings in a collection called the Analects. His teachings had a huge influence on Chinese thought.

Famous Philosophers

Confucius wasn't the only philosopher in ancient China. This period of Zhou history is known as the Hundred Schools era because so many men were teaching their ideas. Here are a few major philosophers and their main concepts.

Mo-Tzu: The simple life is best. Society works best if everyone loves each other. People should do away with wasteful things, such as music, fancy life choices, and warfare. Do whatever benefits the people and the state.

Mencius: Everyone is good by nature. Goodness can be achieved by education and copying the behaviors of moral people. Government must also be moral. If the king behaves well, the people will follow him.

As you listen to the teachers, you notice that one offers a saying of Confucius: "To see what is right and not to do it is lack of courage." When you ask for another, he says: "Virtue is not left to stand alone. He who practices it will have neighbors." You feel honored to hear these special words.

Hsun-tzu: People are naturally evil. Their emotions and needs cause violence and hatred. Education helps overcome this. That's why teachers are very important. Strict laws can also control people.

Laozi: Individuals should be independent. They shouldn't mindlessly obey authority or perform rituals. To achieve inner peace, people must follow the "Dao," which means the path or the way. The Dao will allow people to find their place in nature.

Getting Schooled

After learning how education was important to Confucius, you want to check out the local school. On the way, you pass slaves from other parts of China. No one understands what the slaves are saying, though. They seem to be speaking in foreign languages.

A bearded court minister notices your confusion. He explains that they are speaking **dialects** of Chinese. Each dialect has variations in vocabulary, pronunciation, and grammar. For a Chinese person, figuring out these dialects would be like an English speaker trying to understand someone speaking German or French.

Understanding the Past

Chinese has many different dialects but only one written language. Although Chinese characters have changed over the centuries, people in the 21st century are able to read many ancient writings. That's one reason why Chinese people today feel a strong connection to their ancestors.

你好

hello

謝謝

thank you

再見

goodbye

Speak Now!

Want to speak a few Chinese words and phrases? Try pronouncing these language basics!

hello	ni hao (nee-HOW)
yes	shì (SHE)
no	bù (BOO)
thank you	xièxie (SHE-eh-shih)
goodbye	zàijiàn (ZAH-jee-uhn)

The Write Stuff

You have made it to school and find yourself surrounded by other students. As you sit in class, you learn that Chinese writing doesn't use letters. Instead, each word, or character, is a symbol. Earlier in the Zhou dynasty, the symbols were **pictograms**. For instance, a circle with a line through it was the character for the word *sun*.

But now, characters are **ideograms**—symbols for ideas instead of things. For example, the ideogram for "two" is two straight lines. Now, many characters look less like pictures, and they often indicate how the word is pronounced. You notice that these students are very advanced in writing, so you need to catch up!

After the lesson, the teacher gives you a quiz on pictograms, which are the easiest characters to **decipher**. The first is squiggly lines that resemble branches and roots. Is it *tree*? Yes!

木

DIG DEEPER!

Write On!

The characters on page 23 are from the Zhou period. They are harder to figure out than pictograms. See if you can match the characters to the items below. (The answers are provided on page 32.)

1. 

2. 

3. 

4. 

5. 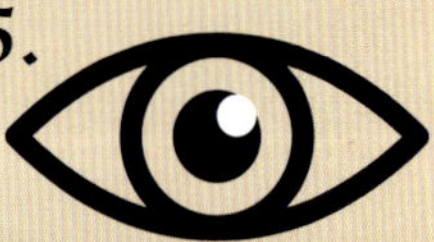

6. 

a. 象

b. 王

c. 鼎

d. 目

e. 口

f. 月

Artful China

Your next lesson is **calligraphy**. The Chinese consider this form of writing the greatest art. The ink is a black, sooty material shaped into a small cake, so you rub the cake against a stone and add water to create an inky liquid. Skilled calligraphers write on silk cloth, but as a beginner, your medium is a piece of wood.

Bamboo Books

In the Zhou era, calligraphers wrote on thin pieces of bamboo, as well as on silk. These bamboo "pages" were connected with strips of leather to form books.

Shine On

Artisans made boxes, statues, and other objects shine with the help of lacquer, which is the sap from the lac tree. They make the sap thin and paint gleaming layers of it over wood and other materials. Lacquer protects the object from wear, water, and insects.

Graduation Day

After a day of classes, a graduating student invites you to his home. He is turning 20, so he is taking part in a capping ceremony to become an adult. An elder member of his clan places the cap on your friend's head, and as an honored guest, you get to choose a "style name" that his friends can call him. He is now a full-fledged noble.

At the house, you run into your friend's sister. She explains that, like all girls, she lives at home learning such skills as cooking and weaving. At age 15, she had a hairpin ceremony, where her hair was tied into a knot and held together by a special hairpin. This ceremony meant that she officially became an adult.

As you walk through your friend's house, you notice it is filled with beautiful Zhou artwork such as silk scrolls painted with landscapes and portraits. Shelves hold gleaming lacquer boxes. Coolest of all is a group of bronze bells that you strike with a mallet to make music. Your friend accompanies on a drum. China is full of surprises!

A Special Land

You've just spent an entire day in ancient China. You've witnessed it up close and personal. Traveling around this country has taught you much. You've discovered a land of conflicts and creativity. It's a place that, though divided by warfare, is united by its written language, ideas from great thinkers, and respect for family and education.

Golden Oldies

Elderly people got a lot of respect in ancient China—and they still do in modern China. A current national law says that children have to take care of a parent who reaches age 60. They are required to visit their elderly folks often and help them with their finances.

Dig It!

Archaeologists are learning even more about ancient China through the artifacts they dig up. Since 1928, scientists have unearthed ancient foundations, tombs, houses, workshops, chariots, bronze vessels—and about 150,000 **oracle bones** covered in writing.

At first, ancient China might have seemed overwhelming. The architecture, clothing, language, food, and customs are unique for first-time visitors. But after exploring China's rich culture, it became easier to understand and appreciate the places you visited—from the busy cities and centers of government to humble farms. You also got to meet some of China's people. You met farmers, kings, teachers, and poets. You got to learn with and from young students and wise scholars. Even though they live different lives from you, you see that you have some things in common. No doubt, the riches of China and its culture will continue to hold great fascination and influence on you and the rest of the world.

Glossary

archaeologists—scientists who deal with past human life by studying historical objects

arduous—very difficult

artisans—people who are skilled at making things by hand

barbarian—of or relating to a foreign land, culture, or people and usually believed to be inferior to another land, culture, or people

bronze—a metal that is made by combining tin and copper

bureaucrat—a person who works for the government

calligraphy—the art of making beautiful handwriting

cavalry—an army component mounted on horseback

Confucianism—a system of ideas and beliefs taught by Confucius

crossbow—a weapon that shoots arrows; consists of a bow attached to a longer piece of wood

decipher—to find the meaning of (something that is difficult to read or understand)

dialects—forms of languages that are spoken in particular areas and that use some of their own words, grammar, and pronunciations

disciples—people who accept and help to spread the teachings of someone

dynasty—a family of leaders who rule over a country for a long period of time; the period of time when a particular dynasty is in power

hemp—a tall Asian plant grown for its tough, woody fiber that is used especially in making rope and cloth

ideograms—pictures or symbols used in writing to represent ideas

infantry—the part of an army that has soldiers who fight on foot

millet—a type of grass that is grown for its seeds, which are used as food

nobleman—a man of high birth or rank

oppressive—cruel or unfair

oracle bones—pieces of turtle shell or bone used for divination

philosopher—a person who studies ideas about knowledge, truth, nature, and the meaning of life

pictograms—pictures in writing that represent objects or things

pillars—large posts that help to hold up things (such as roofs)

scholar—a person who has studied a subject for a long time and knows a lot about it

sovereigns—people who have the highest power and authority

thatched—plant materials (such as straw) used as sheltering covers especially of houses or buildings

vessel—a hollow container for holding liquids

Index

Check It Out!

Books

Allison, Amy. 2000. *The Way People Live: Life in Ancient China*. Lucent Books.

Atkins, Marcie Flinchum. 2015. *Ancient China*. Abdo Publishing.

Chai, May-Lee and Winberg Chai. 2014. *China A to Z*. Plume.

Cotterell, Arthur, 2005. *Ancient China*. DK Publishing.

Fitzgerald, C.P. 2007. *Ancient China*. iBooks, Inc.

Green, Jen, 2006. *China*. National Geographic.

Lin, Grace. 2012. *Starry River of the Sky*. Little, Brown Books for Young Readers.

_____. 2009. *Where the Mountain Meets the Moon*. Little, Brown Books for Young Readers.

Sonneborn, Liz. 2013. *The Ancient World: Ancient China*. Children's Press.

Videos

Lancit, Larry. 2006. *Reading Rainbow: "Liang and the Magic Paintbrush,"* GPN/WNED-TV.

Mei, Hu. 2010. *Confucius*. Mei Ah Entertainment.

Websites

Asia Society. *Chinese Calligraphy*. http://asiasociety.org/chinese-calligraphy

The British Museum. *Ancient China*. http://www.ancientchina.co.uk/menu.html

Try It!

Imagine having the ability to bring one of the great ancient Chinese philosophers mentioned in this book into present day. When you bring him here, you have 24 hours to show him around and learn from him. Plan how you could spend your time with the philosopher of your choice. Decide on the best way to share all the important details of your plan.

- Who would you choose to bring to the present, and why?
- What would you ask the philosopher?
- What places would you take him?
- What types of things would you want to show him? What do you think he would be interested in seeing?
- What do you think his reaction would be to the world today?

About the Author

Born and raised in Brooklyn, New York, Curtis Slepian received a graduate degree in English literature from the University of Michigan. He has worked as an editor at the puzzle magazine *Games*, the kids' science magazine *Contact Kids*, and at *TIME For Kids Learning Ventures*. Among the books he has written are *Animal Adventures 3D, Big Book of How, TIME For Kids United States Atlas*, and *That's Incredible*. He currently lives in New York City, where he enjoys reading books about science and history.

How Do I Say That?

Xia (p. 6) (SHAU)

Zhou (p. 6) (JOE)

Qin (p. 6) (CHIN)

Qu Yuan (p. 16) (chew ih-UU-ahn)

Answers (pp. 22–23)

1. cauldron = c	4. crown = b
2. moon = f	5. eye = d
3. mouth = e	6. elephant = a